Thoughts for Meditation

Secret Place
LIVING

Empowering
you to win in life.
Book 1

DR. SHAUN MARLER

Secret Place Living
by Dr. Shaun Marler

Published by:
World Harvest Ministries, PO Box 90, Bald Hills, Qld, 4036, Australia
www.whm.org.au

This book or parts thereof may not be reproduced in any form, stored in a retrieval system, or transmitted in any form, by any means - electronic, mechanical, photocopy, recording or otherwise - without prior written permission of the author or publisher, except as provided by Australian copyright law.

All scriptural references are taken from the King James Bible unless otherwise stated.

Cover Design by Sarah Freeman

Copyright © Shaun Marler 2022

First Published December 2022

ISBN: 978-0-6450609-5-9

This Book is Dedicated to the Extension of the Kingdom of God.

This book is dedicated to you, the one who desires a deeper walk with God. It is designed to encourage you to live your life out of the 'Secret Place', the place of revelation knowledge.

Every one of us needs to learn how to meditate, feed and build our lives daily on the good Word of God.

In this series of books, you will receive revelations, and kisses from the Father, to empower you to win in life.

Out of intimacy comes great fruitfulness. It is my prayer, that you find your own secret place, to get quiet before God, and listen to the voice of the Spirit as He births life-changing revelations into your heart.

Acknowledgements

When you write a book, it is difficult to acknowledge everyone that has helped you in your life's journey. I just want to thank everyone that has had a positive impact into my life.

One such person was my friend, the late Don Gossett, who encouraged me to write daily. He said, "Shaun, you are anointed for the **write stuff.**"

Because of him, along with others, I have pursued my dream to write daily and publish books. It is my desire to encourage people to never quit and to keep on pursuing their dreams. I also desire, should the Lord tarry, to leave a legacy for others to build upon. May you be inspired by these power thoughts that you find within.

Thank You

I would like to thank all those that have helped me bring this book to completion. Especially Kerrie, for her input and suggestions on editing and presentation. Jeanie Stone for her final proofreading and Sarah Freeman for her cover design and formatting. You guys have helped me publish this book.

Contents

Introduction 13

Power Thought One YOU NEED TO POSSESS GOD! 19

Power Thought Two ON FAITH 21

Power Thought Three ALL THINGS ARE POSSIBLE 23

Power Thought Four ATTITUDE 25

Power Thought Five HOW DO YOU REACT? 27

Power Thought Six DO TODAY'S WORK WELL 29

Power Thought Seven THERE IS NEVER ANY TIME BUT NOW 31

Power Thought Eight TO HAVE FRIENDS, ONE MUST SHOW THEMSELVES FRIENDLY 33

Power Thought Nine UNFORGIVENESS IS DESTRUCTIVE 35

Power Thought Ten I AM NOT MOVED BY WHAT I SEE 37

Power Thought Eleven TEAM WORK MAKES THE DREAM WORK 39

Power Thought Twelve HEART FELT PRAYER 41

Power Thought Thirteen THE USE OF KNOWLEDGE 43

Power Thought Fourteen FEAR OF THE LORD 45

Power Thought Fifteen WALKING IN WISDOM 47

Power Thought Sixteen A TIME OF REST 49

Power Thought Seventeen CHANGE 51

Power Thought Eighteen HOPE 53

Power Thought Nineteen IT IS ALL ON YOU 55

Power Thought Twenty EVERYTHING GOD IS IN IS SUCCESSFUL 57

Power Thought Twenty-One LETTING IT GO! 59

Power Thought Twenty-Two THERE'S NO SUBSTITUTE FOR QUALITY.... 61

Power Thought Twenty-Three WORKING TOWARDS YOUR DREAM....63

Power Thought Twenty-Four REACHING THE ULTIMATE GOAL 65

Power Thought Twenty-Five BEING UNREASONABLE..........................67

Power Thought Twenty-Six C.A.R.E. 69

Power Thought Twenty-Seven WITH TEAMWORK YOU CAN ACHIEVE SO MUCH MORE 71

Power Thought Twenty-Eight DIVINE DESTINY 73

Power Thought Twenty-Nine PROBLEM SOLVED 75

Power Thought Thirty WHERE SHALL WE MEET? 77

Power Thought Thirty-One THY WILL BE DONE 79

Power Thought Thirty-Two ENGAGING OTHERS................................81

Power Thought Thirty-Three JUST BE STILL..83

Power Thought Thirty-Four HONOUR YOUR MAN OF GOD.................85

Power Thought Thirty-Five MOVING ON 87

Power Thought Thirty-Six HIS LOVE 89

Power Thought Thirty-Seven HAVING FAITH TO SEE YOU THROUGH THE TOUGH TIMES 91

Power Thought Thirty-Eight GRATITUDE 93

Power Thought Thirty-Nine GOD NEVER MAKES MISTAKES 95

Power Thought Forty IF IT'S UNACCEPTABLE, DON'T ACCEPT IT....97

Power Thought Forty-One DIVINE INTERRUPTIONS..........................99

Power Thought Forty-Two COME APART BEFORE YOU COME APART . 101

Power Thought Forty-Three GOD'S SPIRIT KNOWS - LOOK BEFORE YOU LEAP 103

Power Thought Forty-Four WE MUST DECREASE SO HE CAN INCREASE ... 105

Power Thought Forty-Five BORN TWICE, DIE ONCE 107

Power Thought Forty-Six WORDS, WORDS, WORDS 109

Power Thought Forty-Seven TAKE ANOTHER DRINK 111

Power Thought Forty-Eight DESTINY IS A CHOICE 113

Power Thought Forty-Nine AGAINST THE ODDS 115

Power Thought Fifty EVERY TOMORROW HAS TWO HANDLES 117

Power Thought Fifty-One FAITH IS NEEDED FOR THE IMPOSSIBLE 119

Power Thought Fifty-Two FAITH 121

Power Thought Fifty-Three SUCCESS IN LIFE 123

Power Thought Fifty-Four BELIEVE 125

Power Thought Fifty-Five DESIRE THE MILK OF THE WORD 127

Power Thought Fifty-Six DO THE FEARED JOBS FIRST! 129

Power Thought Fifty-Seven FIRST SEEK THE KINGDOM OF GOD 131

Power Thought Fifty-Eight YOU HAVE THE CAPACITY TO THINK BIG ... 133

Power Thought Fifty-Nine GOD MEETS ALL YOUR NEEDS 135

Power Thought Sixty YOUR BEST IS YET TO COME 137

SECRET PLACE LIVING

INTRODUCTION

"He that dwelleth in the secret place of the most High shall abide under the shadow of the Almighty. I will say of the Lord, He is my refuge and my fortress: my God; in him will I trust" (Psalm 91:1-2).

The title of my book, 'Secret Place Living,' is inspired by the above scripture from God's Word. We can see here from verse 1 that the person who dwells, which means to sit, remain, dwell or abide in the Secret Place of the Most High, is afforded the protection and shelter of the Almighty God.

God wants you to win in life through His Son, the Lord Jesus Christ and the victory He won for you through the Cross of Calvary. He died and rose again to give us His life and His peace. The life that He has now given to us through His Spirit and Word is superior in quality and overflowing in quantity. God wants you to have this abundant life!

"The thief comes not, but for to steal, and to kill, and to destroy: I am come that they might have life, and that they might have it more abundantly" (John 10:10).

I like to say that the secret place of the Most High God is the place of revelation knowledge.

There are revelations that have been hidden, in Christ, in God for you. These revelations are to be found in God's Word. As we take time aside each day to read, meditate and think about God's Word, allowing the Holy Spirit to birth understanding into our heart or spirit of this Word, we are equipped to win in life.

In the Song of Solomon 1 verse 1.

> *"The song of songs, which is Solomon's. Let him kiss me with the kisses of his mouth: for thy love is better than wine"* (Song of Solomon 1:1-2).

The word 'kiss' here in the Hebrew is the Word 'nashaq'. This is a very interesting word, and as you study the 'root' of this word, it comes from an idea or meaning to kiss, or to equip with weapons, equipped for battle, to be armed. When God kisses us, He equips us for battle, and arms us with weapons. The Word of God tells us that the weapons of our warfare are not carnal but mighty through God to the pulling down of strongholds, bringing into captivity every thought and wicked imaginations to the obedience of Christ. (2 Corinthians 10:4-5 paraphrased).

A wicked imagination, is a thought designed to defeat you. It is designed to take you from your destiny in one way or another. It comes from the enemy to harm, hinder or destroy your progress in life. It's born of fear and not of faith.

A revelation is a kiss from God that equips us or arms us for spiritual battle and life. We read above, the thief or the enemy comes to kill, steal and destroy. This starts in the battleground of our mind, in our thought life. We know, from the book of Proverbs 23:7, that as a man thinks in his heart, so is he. I like to say, what we think in our heart, so we become. What we think in our heart or mind, comes to pass in time. I did a study on this verse once, and in a nutshell, I learnt that the natural mind is the gatekeeper to the subconscious mind, the mind of the Spirit. Jesus said, *"Out of the abundance of heart, the mouth speaks."* He also said in Matthew 4:4, *"But he answered and said, It is written, Man shall not live by bread alone, but by every word that proceeds out of the mouth of God."*

We can live, thrive and walk in victory, through God's Word. As we meditate, dwell on and in, mutter, speak God's Word, we will be creating the kind of life that we want. The life that Jesus Christ gave Himself for, for us to have.

God's Holy Spirit kisses us with a revelation and brings to life God's Word. The Holy Spirit causes the written Word to become a Rhema word.

A living word, that equips you for battle in the circumstances you are currently facing.

One day King David woke up, and as he got out of bed, the Bible recalls, he asked himself a question: *"Why are you cast down oh my soul and why are you troubled within me?"* (Psalms 42:5). We can see from reading this Psalm that his enemies were giving him a hard time, and he was being plagued with the thought "where is God?" David was being bombarded in his thought life that God had left him. What was his solution? IT was again to praise God and, by so doing, filling his mind with positive affirmations of God's presence, power, ability, and love.

We are to speak out these revelations, positive affirmations that have been birthed in our spirit by the Spirit of God, from God's Word. As we do, we frame our world with the Word of God. The Bible reveals that death and life are in the power of our tongue.

Secret place living is about abiding in the Word of God and allowing the Word of God to abide in you.

Whatever circumstance you are facing, God has an answer. The Spirit of God will give you a word in season, to empower you to win in life, through Jesus Christ.

As I have meditated on God's Word over the years, and built it down into my spirit, I have found that in times of need, a thought, a scripture, or an idea has been brought to mind.

I believe this is the working of the Holy Spirit in my life, bringing to my remembrance what Jesus has taught me, through His Word.

Over the years, I have loved to collect great quotes from others as well as writing them myself. These quotes have been like an injection of enthusiasm, a push when times were tough, an inspiration, a thought that "I could do it" if I did not quit. They have been an attitude check and much, much more. They have helped me immensely on my journey to success. They have encapsulated opinions, ideas and dreams, provided a supercharged thought to blast doubt out of my life and propel me on my way. They have been a gem and a word in season, when I was weary and have helped me be an "Up" person, in a "down" kind of world.

I encourage every one of you to have a 'secret place', a place where you go to each day to have a quiet time with the Lord, a place where you can become intimate with God, by becoming intimate with His Word. Allowing the Holy Spirit to kiss you and bring revelation and faith to your heart, mind and life. To give you thoughts and words that you can speak forth in confidence and power.

I pray that this book and this devotional series helps you and inspires you, giving you a place to start your deeper journey into

God's love plan for your life. May you receive many kisses (revelations) from God that equip you for victory in life. I now leave you with this scripture in Jeremiah 29:11 (NIV) as you use this book to begin and continue your exciting journey of living in the secret place.

> *"For I know the plans I have for you," declares the Lord,*
> *"plans to prosper you and not to harm you,*
> *plans to give you hope and a future."*

Power Thought One

YOU NEED TO POSSESS GOD!

"The more you possess God, the more you are made like Him!"
-Jeanne Guyon, Grenoble, France (1685)-

I love this statement by Jeanne Guyon. In life there are so many things that try to possess us, take our attention, fill our time - some good, others not so good. We must remember to seek first the Kingdom of God and His righteousness, God will then add to your life all the other things that people seek after. God wants to bless us and give us nice things to enjoy. He just doesn't want those things coming before Him or taking over our lives. Some people are so possessed by material things, that these things control their lives.

Families are wrecked and relationships destroyed sometimes, because someone has become so possessive of certain things that they put these things before everyone else in their lives, even their children or spouse. The Bible says that the love of money (not money, but the craving desire or love of it) is the root of all evil. Possess God so there is not room in your heart for anything else to take your affection. Then love God, your family and all others from out of the love you now possess - for God is love.

Empowering you to win in life through Jesus Christ.

Power Thought Two

On Faith

"Faith is the ability to see the invisible and believe the incredible, and that is what enables believers to receive the impossible."
-Dr. Shaun Marler-

Hebrews 11:1 tells us, *"Now faith is the substance of things hoped for the evidence of things not yet seen."* God has great things in store for your life today, believe to see the goodness of God in the land of the living. Commit your ways to God; seek Him first everyday and He will make straight your path.

Empowering you to win in life through Jesus Christ.

POWER THOUGHT THREE

ALL THINGS ARE POSSIBLE

*"If you can believe it, you can achieve it,
but you must add steam to your dream."*
-Dr. Shaun Marler-

The Bible tells us all things are possible to those who believe, but the Bible definition of 'believe' is sometimes different to people's definitions. To believe here means to have faith. We are to have faith in God and His ability, in us to bring things to pass. It means to entrust, to commit (to trust). It's not just a passive word, but rather an active word.

It is an action, faith is an act, *"be doers of the Word, not hearers only!"*. Have confidence in God, that He is able to perform that which He has promised. You must do something - add some steam to your dream, be proactive, walk towards it, work towards it.

Do your part and let God do His - we do the possible and God does the impossible!

GOOD THINGS ARE COMING
GOOD THINGS ARE COMING
GOOD THINGS ARE COMING
GOOD THINGS ARE COMING
GOOD THINGS ARE COMING
GOOD THINGS ARE COMING
GOOD THINGS ARE COMING

Empowering you to win in life through Jesus Christ.

Power Thought Four

ATTITUDE

"Your attitude in life determines your altitude."
-Dr. Shaun Marler-

If you want to fly high in life and achieve great things, then your attitude is the one all-important thing that will determine whether you will succeed or fail. In every plane there is an altitude gauge and an attitude gauge. The altitude gauge determines how high you are flying while the attitude gauge determines how you are flying in relation to the horizon. How are you flying today in relation to your horizon (your destination, your goal, your vision, your dream)? Are you on track or have you drifted off course? Are you flying upside down or skewiff? Check your attitude.

"He maketh my feet like hinds' feet, and setteth me upon my high places" (Psalm 18:33).

I dare you right now to stop and have an attitude check. Do you have the right attitude to reach your dream, your goal, your destination, or are you going to crash? Remember, *"Your attitude in life determines whether you will reach your dreams."*

Empowering you to win in life through Jesus Christ.

Power Thought Five

HOW DO YOU REACT?

"Outlook determines outcome, and attitude determines action"
-Dr. Shaun Marler-

David in the Bible, who was called to be King, discovered that what was important was not the circumstances around him but the attitude within him. If he was to reach his God given goals and fulfil his destiny, then he was going to have to watch his attitude towards life. He was going to have to have some attitude checks along the way.

Check his attitude to see what happened to him, watch his action or reactions to others - how he would act when he was treated unfairly. Would he love, forgive, forget, and move forward, or would he retaliate, hold and bear grudges, allow unforgiveness in his heart? How would he react towards his superiors, his wife, family, friends and peers? Would he set an example for others to follow? How would he react when God judged him, corrected him and dealt with him? Would he repent and turn back to God, making restitution where possible or would he get bitter, harden his heart towards God, go on in his rebellion and strike out at others? Would he follow Saul's example or God's Word?

If your life is falling apart, it is likely that you are part of the problem. We have seen that unbelief and rebellion only lead to emptiness. You can continue to tear things apart with your bad attitude, or you can change your life for the better by submitting to God and allowing Him to work.

> *"But now thy kingdom shall not continue: the Lord hath sought him a man after his own heart, and the Lord hath commanded him to be captain over his people, because thou hast not kept that which the Lord commanded thee"* (1 Samuel 13:14).

I dare you to not be like Saul, but to be like David and go after the heart of God!

Empowering you to win in life through Jesus Christ.

Power Thought Six

DO TODAY'S WORK WELL

"Either you run the day or the day runs you."
-Jim Rohn-

Now there's a thought for the day. If we take care of the minutes and the hours, the days and weeks will take care of themselves. You can only act where you are now. There is never any time but NOW! You cannot act where you are not, you cannot act where you have not been, and you cannot act where you are going to be. You can act only where you are.

Don't bother as to whether yesterday's work was done well or not. Don't live in the mistakes of yesterday, just do today's work well. Do not try to do tomorrow's work today; there will be plenty of time to do it tomorrow, when you get to it.

> *Jesus said, "Therefore do not worry about tomorrow, for tomorrow will worry about it's own things. Sufficient for the day is its own trouble"* (Matthew 6:34 (NKJV).

Do not wait for a change in circumstances before you act, but change your circumstances through action. If you want something you have never had, you will have to do something you have never done! SO act now, by doing today's work well, and believe that your action will bring about the change in circumstances you desire.

Empowering you to win in life through Jesus Christ.

Power Thought Seven

THERE IS NEVER ANY TIME BUT NOW

"Faith is an act."
-Smith Wigglesworth-

The Bible says that, *"Now faith is the substance of things hoped for the evidence of things not seen"* (Hebrews 11:1). Now is the only time we have, so then we must act now. Do not wait for a change in the environment before you act, get a change of environment by action.

Act in faith NOW, faith is always in the NOW! It is never off in the far distant future. Hold to the one vision of what you want and act now. Smith Wigglesworth said, *"Faith is an act"*, it requires action.

Faith (the Bible says), without works is dead, being alone. We could say, *"faith without corresponding actions is dead."* The time to act is now – there is never any time like the present. Take action now. You can act by faith upon the environment in which you are now, to cause yourself to be transferred to a better environment.

SECRET PLACE LIVING

Empowering you to win in life through Jesus Christ.

Power Thought Eight

TO HAVE FRIENDS, ONE MUST SHOW THEMSELVES FRIENDLY

"Value others by valuing their point of view."
-Dr. Shaun Marler-

Spend quality time with family and friends, especially your children. But remember, quality time will never make up for too little time. The Hebrew word for 'children' means builder of the family name. We should train up our children in the way we want them to go. Training involves spending time with them, teaching them, mentoring them, showing how to do things (not just telling them). It means leading by example, being a role model for your children. It also requires understanding, putting yourself in their shoes and taking the time to listen. Listening requires patience and a humble attitude - we as people have often lost the art of listening.

We are so busy making our point or trying to get our point across, that we often don't hear the other's point of view. We are just waiting for them to shut up so we can have our say. In doing this we haven't respected the other person - they don't feel valued by us, they don't feel like we care, and so often walls start to be put up and people's relationships break down.

"A man who has friends must himself be friendly, But there is a friend who sticks closer than a brother "(Proverbs 18:24).

Let's value others by valuing their point of view, showing them respect by taking the time to listen. Let's build bridges, not barriers, by showing ourselves friendly. Let's regain the lost art of communication by learning to listen.

Empowering you to win in life through Jesus Christ.

Power Thought Nine

Unforgiveness Is Destructive

"To violate the law of love is to live in unforgiveness."
-Sunday Adelaja-

A word of faith, a word of revelation from God's Word to your heart, revealed by the Holy Spirit can change your life.

Now let's think for a moment about this thought. Unforgiveness in the heart, produces negative and destructive thoughts in the mind. The Bible tells us as a man thinks in his heart, so is he. I like to say, "and so he becomes!" What you think about and see in your mind comes to pass in time.

Unforgiveness is a violation of grace. If we allow unforgiveness to dwell in our hearts, this will produce these negative, destructive thoughts in our minds which will ultimately affect us in a negative way.

Maybe a root of bitterness will be formed in us. This in turn will affect our attitudes and be seen and felt by those around us. In addition to this, dwelling on these bitter thoughts of unforgiveness, will produce chemicals of a destructive nature in us. As these are released into our system, our health will be affected in some way.

"I call heaven and earth as witnesses today against you, that I have set before you life and death, blessing and cursing; therefore choose life, that both you and your descendants may live;" (Deuteronomy 30:19).

I dare you today to forgive those who may have disappointed you in any way. Release them in your mind and think happy thoughts of love, joy, and peace.

Empowering you to win in life through Jesus Christ.

Power Thought Ten

I Am Not Moved By What I See

*"I am not moved by what I see. I am not moved by what I feel.
I am only moved by what I believe."*
-Smith Wigglesworth-

If God's Word says you are forgiven, then you are forgiven, if God's Word says your needs are met, then your needs are met. If God's Word says you are healed, you are healed. If you don't let go of God's Word, but keep it in your heart and mouth, then you can't lose.

There is no force the devil can bring against you that can overthrow the Word of God. God's Word will make you a victor every time. So if you have been wanting good success and it has been eluding you, quit wondering if you have what it takes to succeed and remember instead, who lives in you. Then turn to the Word and put God's success formula to work in your life. Start talking it, start thinking it, start doing it! You can believe all day long that the Bible is true- and that's to your credit- but what the Bible says will never affect your life in a personal way until you start acting on God's Word.

Do not worry or fret that God has given more faith to others than He has to you. Rest assured in the fact that God has imparted enough faith to you to make sure you are covered from head to toe! Faith counts the thing done, before anything has happened. Remember, no promise of God can fail to be fulfilled.

"For with God nothing will be impossible" (Luke 1:37).

I dare you today to believe and confess this scripture!

Empowering you to win in life through Jesus Christ.

Power Thought Eleven

Team Work Makes the Dream Work

"Together everyone achieves more."
-Unknown-

Behind every great leader there is a great team of committed individuals who are playing their part, sacrificing time and energy, to propel their team and leader to success. No one ever accomplished anything great on their own. Through synergy and the combining of efforts and ideas, our strengths and resources are multiplied. If we make an acronym out of the word TEAM we can say, *"Together Everyone Achieves More."*

The Bible speaks much on the power of unity. One can put a thousand to flight, and two, ten thousand. Recruit like-minded people to be part of your team, or become a part of a team so together you can achieve a worthwhile dream.

"Behold, how good and how pleasant it is, for brethren to dwell together in unity!" (Psalm 133:1).

I dare you today to be a productive part of winning team.

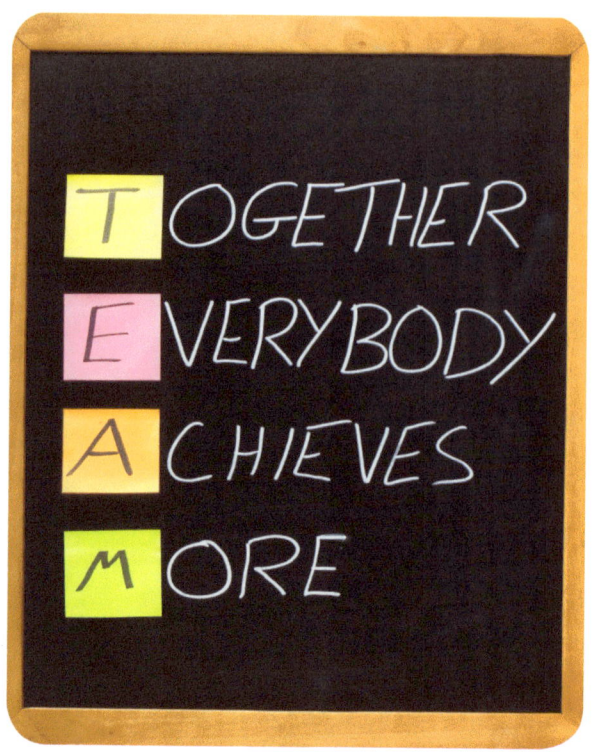

Empowering you to win in life through Jesus Christ.

Power Thought Twelve

Heart Felt Prayer

"When you pray, pray so that your heart will feel the emotions of your prayers, so then God's heart will feel those prayers."
-Dr. Shaun Marler-

Pray heart felt prayer, pray without ceasing, pray the Word. You must feel the passion in your prayers. In a intimate moment with a loved one as you share the passion or emotion of that moment, they (the other person) feel it and so do you. Your words become you, the essence of yourself, your life, energy, love and feelings are expressed in your own heart felt words. You become your words. God and His Word are one. God's Word to me, is God in all His fullness to me. God does not speak idle words. He watches over His word to perform it. He has framed Himself in his words.

In the Beginning was the Word, and the Word was with God and the Word was God.

"The earnest (heartfelt, continued) prayer of a righteous man makes tremendous power available (dynamic in it's working)" (James 5v16b, Amplified Bible).

Empowering you to win in life through Jesus Christ.

Power Thought Thirteen

THE USE OF KNOWLEDGE

"Wisdom is the right use of knowledge. To know is not to be wise. Many men know a great deal, and are all the greater fools for it. There is no fool so great a fool as a knowing fool. But to know how to use knowledge is to have wisdom."
-Charles Haddon Spurgeon-
-English Preacher (1834-1892)-

They say that knowledge is power, but as the Bible says, *"knowledge can also puff one up."* The incorrect use of knowledge can be very destructive to others and also to ourselves.

As Spurgeon pointed out, wisdom is the ability to use knowledge correctly, for the benefit of ourselves and others.

"The fear of the Lord is the beginning of knowledge, but fools despise wisdom and instruction" (Proverbs 1:7).

I dare you today to get wisdom, ask God for wisdom, ask in faith and the Father will give you the wisdom that you seek (James 1:5-6).

"Wisdom is the principal thing; Therefore get wisdom. And in all your getting, get understanding. Exalt her, and she will promote you; She will bring you honor, when you embrace her. She will place on your head an ornament of grace; A crown of glory she will deliver to you. Hear, my son, and receive my sayings, And the years of your life will be many" (Proverbs 4:7-10).

I dare you to meditate on these verses from the book of Proverbs.

Empowering you to win in life through Jesus Christ.

Power Thought Fourteen

Fear of the Lord

"The fear of the Lord is the beginning of knowledge, but fools despise wisdom and instruction."
-Proverbs 1:7 NKJV-

"Come, you children, listen to me; I will teach you the fear of the Lord. Who is the man who desires life, and loves many days, that he may see good? Keep your tongue from evil, and your lips from speaking deceit. Depart from evil and do good; Seek peace and pursue it. The eyes of the Lord are on the righteous, and His ears are open to their cry. The face of the Lord is against those who do evil, To cut off the remembrance of them from the earth. The righteous cry out, and the Lord hears, and delivers them out of all their troubles. The Lord is near to those who have a broken heart, and saves such as have a contrite spirit. Many are the afflictions of the righteous, but the Lord delivers him out of them all" (Psalm 34:11-19).

Empowering you to win in life through Jesus Christ.

Power Thought Fifteen

Walking in Wisdom

"If you correct your mind the rest of your life will fall into place."
-Unknown-

It has been said that we are what we eat. It is so important what we feed our minds. The words and the thoughts that we meditate on today are shaping us and our future world.

In His Word God has given us the book of Proverbs. There are 31 chapters in this book. I like to think God gave us one chapter for everyday of the month. I dare you today to read a portion each day from the book of Proverbs for the next 31 days.

> *"Trust in the Lord with all your heart, and lean not on your own understanding; In all your ways acknowledge Him, and He shall direct your paths"* (Proverbs 3:5-6).

Empowering you to win in life through Jesus Christ.

Power Thought Sixteen

A TIME OF REST

"Come apart, before you come apart."
-Dr. Shaun Marler-

"Ours is a complicated, cluttered world", writes Chuck Swindoll in his book, 'Intimacy with the Almighty'. *"God did not create it that way! Depraved restless humanity has made it that way!"*

Jesus tells us to close the door to the noise and hurry of busy 21st century life. Find a 'closet' and shut the door! You choose a time and a place that is best for you. The only requirement is separation from the noise and confusion of life. You must come apart and rest awhile. You must let God refresh and renew your spirit; you must rest and recharge your batteries. For if you do not come apart and rest, you will eventually come apart - there will be a system break down somewhere.

That's why when God created man, He instituted the Sabbath's day rest! *"Come apart, before you come apart."*

> *"And he said unto them, "Come you yourselves apart into a desert place, and rest a while:" for there were many coming and going, and they had no leisure so much as to eat"* (Mark 6:31).

I dare you to take time to allow God to inspire, speak, fill and recharge your batteries for you.

Empowering you to win in life through Jesus Christ.

Power Thought Seventeen

CHANGE

"Change is inevitable, growth is intentional."
-Dr. Shaun Marler-

Change is a law of life, and those who look only to the past or present are certain to miss the future. Change is never easy to accept. We have to approach it with a positive mental attitude. If you lived 100 years ago you probably would have been a farmer, miner, or possibly some sort of factory worker. 100 years ago these vocations made up 90% of the work force. Very few people worked behind a desk.

If someone said back then that *"100 years from now, farmers will only make up 1.5% of the workforce, miners about the same and factory workers 10%,"* you may have replied, *"well what could the other people possibly be doing?"*

Change, our world has changed so much in the last 100 years. It is amazing that technology has allowed us to increase productivity to this extent. What will technology bring us in the next 100 years? Our world is constantly changing, it's inevitable. Change is a law of life - everything is in a constant state of change, even if to our natural eye it is too slow to detect or perceive.

God and His Word are the only constants in the universe. The Lord says, *"I change not!"* (Malachi 3:6). God is already perfect – perfect love, perfect wisdom, and perfect goodness. You and I, and the rest of creation, are in a state of change. It often takes more courage to change one's opinion than to stick to it. When you blame others you give up your power to change. Change is inevitable but growth is intentional.

I dare you to make a decision today, to grow and learn in our forever-changing environment and world. Let's grow in God, let's grow in the Word and let's become all that God has destined us to become.

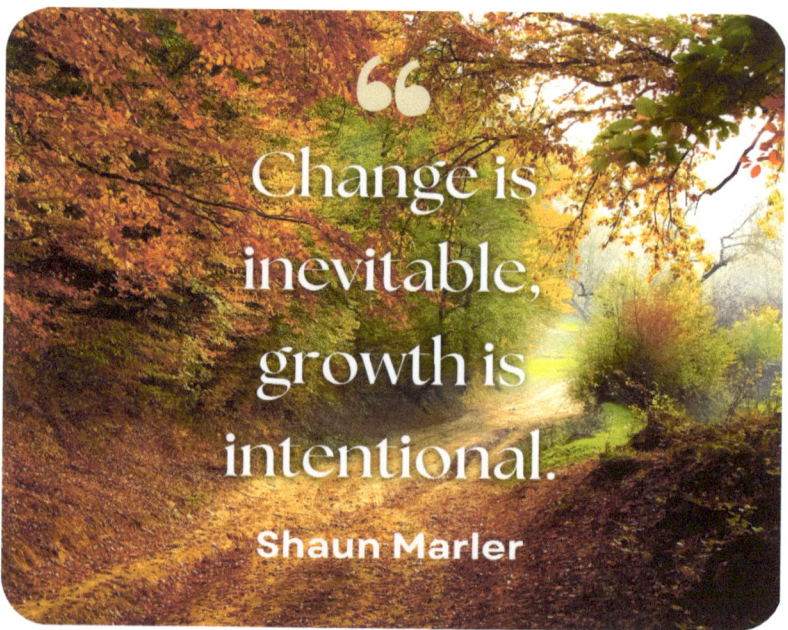

Empowering you to win in life through Jesus Christ.

Power Thought Eighteen

HOPE

"Where there is life there is hope."
-Frank Marler-

My Dad always said, *"where there is life there is hope."* Believe in a better day. I believe there is a better day for you, this is not the end. Struggle is the evidence that you are not defeated, so don't you quit. Keep going, get up, you can win.

You might be knocked down but you are not knocked out – get up my friend and finish the bout. There are great rewards for those who do not quit. Quitters never win. Winners never quit. Be persistent, you are a winner, you were made by God. Your best is yet to come.

Napoleon the great military general said, *"All great leaders are dealers in hope."* We need to give people hope. Abraham, the Word recalls, believed in hope against all hope, and became the father of many nations. You can do it in Christ, you are Abraham's seed, and a recipient of all the promises of God.

> *"For I know the thoughts that I think toward you, saith the Lord, thoughts of peace, and not of evil, to give you an expected end"* (Jeremiah 29:11).

My friend I tell you today, your best is yet to come. It is going to get better, only believe. Stand strong and see the salvation of God.

Empowering you to win in life through Jesus Christ.

Power Thought Nineteen

IT IS ALL ON YOU

"No one can make you feel inferior without your consent."
-Eleanor Roosevelt-

I love this saying by Eleanor Roosevelt. Think about it – you know there are people out there who just love to put you down. They have nothing better to do with their time than to tell you how bad you are doing. My Dad always said, *"If you can't say a good word about someone, don't say a bad one."*

The Word of God tells us to let our words impart grace and faith to the hearers (Eph. 4:29). Even though people can say all kinds of things, it is really up to us how we react to such remarks. It is up to us if we allow these thoughts to hinder our progress in life. Will we be crippled by these things, feeling inferior all our lives because someone, maybe a teacher, a peer, a superior or a family member once held a thought about us or said words that put us down?

Or will we rise above them, proving the other wrong, overcoming thoughts of inferiority, knowing we were made by God for a purpose, for a reason. Remember that *"you are a somebody – you were made by God."*

Give no consent to thoughts of inferiority living in your head.

I dare you to *"give no consent to things that are living in your head that are belittling you in any way."* Remember, you are a somebody, and God has a plan for your life that is all good!

Empowering you to win in life through Jesus Christ.

Power Thought Twenty

Everything God Is In Is Successful

*"This is the day which the Lord hath made;
we will rejoice and be glad in it."*
-Psalm 118:24-

Invite God into your life and affairs today – commit your way to Him. Trust also in Him and He will bring it to pass, He will make it good. Don't ignore God, communicate with Him, talk with Him, and walk with Him.

As you talk to God He will talk to you. As you walk with God He will walk with you. Love God, because He first loved you and proved His love to you by sending Jesus to die for you. Remember, *"everything God is in is successful"* so make sure that the thing you are in, God is in.

Everything God is in is successful. I dare you to allow Jesus to get involved in your daily life by becoming a daily worshipper of Him.

Empowering you to win in life through Jesus Christ.

Power Thought Twenty-One

LETTING IT GO!

"When you resent someone, they live rent-free in your head."
-Unknown-

I don't know who the anonymous person was who said this, but don't you just love it? The word resent means *"to feel or show displeasure or indignation at, from a sense of injury or insult, to take ill or feel resentment, to express or exhibit displeasure or indignation by words or acts."*

If we resent someone enough, this person will live rent-free in our head, we will be wasting precious thought, energy and time, dwelling on past hurts this person may have caused us. In so doing we will carry this person around with us wherever we go. I don't know about you, but I can say that if I had to carry someone around all day, by the end of it I would be very tired. That is how it is if we allow resentment to dwell in our minds. We will become stressed and tired. We need to set them free by forgiving and in so doing we will free ourselves.

The Word says in Hebrews 12:15, *"not to allow roots of bitterness to spring up in us, which only result in others in our lives being defiled."* We need to repent of and forsake any resentments we feel towards others lest we eventually hurt ourselves as well.

Power Thought Twenty-Two

There's No Substitute For Quality

> *"And whatsoever ye do, do it heartily,
> as to the Lord, and not unto men."*
> ***-Colossians 3:23-***

My wife and I have learned in life that there is no substitute for quality. Quality means *"having a high degree of excellence, an inherent and distinguishing characteristic, essential character, superiority of a kind."*

We need to put quality into everything we do. My Dad always said, *"If a job is worth doing it is worth doing properly."* In life we should look for quality – the old saying, *"you get what you pay for"* is sometimes true. The cheapest is not always the best, it may not last. Then again, the dearest is not always the best either.

Look for quality and at the same time put quality into everything you do. Spend quality time with your family. Give your work in life (your vocation) your best, put in your best effort. Give God your best, put quality into what you do. We only pass this way but once, so let's do our best.

Empowering you to win in life through Jesus Christ.

Power Thought Twenty-Three

WORKING TOWARDS YOUR DREAM

"You have to stay awake to make dreams come true."
-Dr. Shaun Marler-

Many people dream of worthwhile accomplishments, while others stay awake and work on them to make them come true. The Bible says in Ecclesiastes 5:3, *"the dream cometh through a multitude of business."*

We must dream, but then we must add sweat, effort, and supply work to the dream to bring it to pass. The word multitude in the above scripture means excellent, increase, more abundance. We must put excellent, worthwhile effort and energy into our dreams.

Put some action into your dreams, do something, take a positive step towards your dream. If you are not sure how, enlist others into your dream, ask their advice. Find someone who has done something great and ask them to mentor you. But in doing this, make sure they are people who believe in your dream, and are achievers themselves.

Don't just get "yes" men either – you need people who will point out possible pitfalls as well. Remember as the Word says, in the abundance of counsel there is safety.

Empowering you to win in life through Jesus Christ.

Power Thought Twenty-Four

REACHING THE ULTIMATE GOAL

"Difficulties are stepping stones on the way to success."
-Dr. Shaun Marler-

Jesus said, *"in this world you will have tribulation (problems, temptations, tests, and trials), but be of good cheer for I have overcome the world"* (John 16:33).

Jesus has paid the full price for your victory, your success in life. The road to success is full of highlights, joys, rewards and other pleasures, but it is also has more than its fair share of problems, challenges and difficulties. Don't let these difficulties become stumbling blocks that discourage you from going any further. Don't allow these problems to get you down or make you quit or give up. Don't throw in the towel.

Instead, realize that these very problems are your stepping stones on your journey to success. As each one is overcome your confidence grows, your experience increases, and you understand more. You have applied knowledge and you have grown, you have learned, you have another victory and a testimony.

You are now one step closer to your ultimate goal. These very problems that you are facing are your stepping stones. You can do it, you can win. Jesus is on your side and if God be for you, who can be against you.

Empowering you to win in life through Jesus Christ.

Power Thought Twenty-Five

Being Unreasonable

"The reasonable man adapts himself to the world; the unreasonable one persists in trying to adapt the world to himself. Therefore all progress depends on the unreasonable man."
-George Bernard Shaw-

Unreasonable means *"not governed by reason, exceeding reasonable limits, going beyond accepted or reasonable limits."* Jesus was an unreasonable man, He went beyond what our natural minds could comprehend. He walked in, moved in, and lived in the miraculous.

He did unreasonable things, with just five loaves and two fishes – He fed the multitude of people. Jesus walked on water, restored sight to the man born blind, by faith He brought healing and deliverance to all that came to Him.

Jesus was not limited to (or by) His circumstances; He served a limitless God, fulfilling the Father's Will to the max. The Bible tells us how God was In Christ reconciling the world unto Himself, not imputing their transgressions unto them, and has given unto us the Word of reconciliation (2 Corinthians 5:19).

The Word says in Romans 12:2, *"be not conformed to this world but be ye transformed by the renewing of your mind."*

I dare you, in a good sense, to be unreasonable and do unreasonable things. Go on, you can do it, you can win, go and change your world for the better with the love and power of God.

Empowering you to win in life through Jesus Christ.

Power Thought Twenty-Six

C.A.R.E.

"Bear ye one another's burdens, and so fulfil the law of Christ."
-Galatians 6:2-

       C – Care
       A – And
       R – Reach
       E – Everyone!

We would do well to remember the acronym C.A.R.E. The Bible tells us to watch out for each other, pray for each other, and be other-minded by bearing one another's burdens.

All of life's successes come from initiating relationships with the right people. For example, by networking and then strengthening those relationships, using good people skills. One of the keys for winning in life is building good strategic relationships, but let it be a win-win situation, not just the attitude of *"what can I get out of this relationship"*. Instead, we need to have the attitude of *"what can I put into this relationship to bless the other party"*.

I dare you to build strategic relationships. I dare you to be a blessing to somebody this day.

Empowering you to win in life through Jesus Christ.

Power Thought Twenty-Seven

With Teamwork You Can Achieve So Much More

"Individuals play the game, teams win the victories."
-*John C Maxwell*-

I love this quote by leading author John C Maxwell. We need to build teams. Teams maximize a leader's potential, and minimizes their weaknesses. Teams share the credit for victories and the blame for losses. This fosters genuine humility and real community.

In contrast, when individuals take credit or blame alone, this fosters pride and sometimes a sense of failure. Teams can simply do more than an individual. If you want to reach your potential, or strive for the seemingly impossible – such as communicating your message two thousand years after you are gone, then you will have to become a team player.

As John Maxwell says, individuals play the game, but teams win the Victories.

Empowering you to win in life through Jesus Christ.

Power Thought Twenty-Eight

Divine Destiny

"Believe in your divine destiny, step by faith into what God has for your life."
-Dr. Shaun Marler-

One day God dropped this powerful thought into my life, *"Shaun believe in your divine destiny, see yourself in God's will for your life, see yourself fulfilling the call to which you are called, by seeing yourself doing those things I have called you to."*

See yourself in your future in God. We are drawn to our dominant thinking patterns. Also our mind does not think in words, it thinks in pictures! Therefore we must hold a picture in our mind of where we want to be and what we want to do. We must see ourselves doing those things we dream about and hold these thought pictures in our mind.

What we see in our mind will come to pass in time. We must believe that our God is able. He is able to perfect that, or fulfil that, which concerns us. We do our part, and God works behind the scenes doing His. This day, believe that God is for you and not against you. Believe in your future in God, believe in your divine destiny.

I dare you to believe today that you can do all things through Christ!

"I can do all things through Christ which strengthens me" (Philippians 4:13).

Empowering you to win in life through Jesus Christ.

Power Thought Twenty-Nine

PROBLEM SOLVED

"No problem is without a solution."
-Kerrie Marler-

The Bible says in Mark 9:23, *"All things are possible to them that believe"*. My Dad always used to say, *"Where there is a will, there is a way."*

Jesus has a way for you! He is "the Way", "the Truth", and "the Life." I ask you a question: *"Have you prayed today, to find that way?"* Jesus is the Way, for your way. He is The Truth, The Reality. Jesus is real, He will be with you in times of trouble. Call upon Him, for while He is near He will help you.

No problem is without a solution. You can give your way back, seed your way back into any relationship. I dare you today to pray and seek God for the answer you need to your problem. Remember, where there is a will there is a way. Go on you can do it, you can win! Open your heart to God today as He is your solution, He is your Answer!

He will show you, and lead you in the way.

Empowering you to win in life through Jesus Christ.

POWER THOUGHT THIRTY

WHERE SHALL WE MEET?

"But thou, when thou prayest, enter into thy closet, and when thou hast shut thy door, pray to thy Father which is in secret; and thy Father which seeth in secret shall reward thee openly."
-Matthew 6:6-

When Jesus talks about closet, He doesn't mean one full of shoes, clothing or other kinds of clutter. The Greek word for closet here is tameon, it refers to the place in the Old Testament temple where the treasures are stored. It is a place of devotions where the riches are received.

Jesus isn't specifying one place to seek the Father. More important than the word "closet' is the phrase "shut the door!" Shut the door from the noise and cares of daily life. Wherever your closet may be, such as field, room, rooftop, park, or some other quiet place. A place where you can get alone with God to commune with Him, love Him, and most importantly listen to Him.

I dare you to find your 'secret place' and there spend time with God each day. Learn to live your life by fellowshipping with Him and His Word, out of this secret place.

Remember if you talk to God, He will talk to you. If you commune with God, He will commune with you.

Empowering you to win in life through Jesus Christ.

Power Thought Thirty-One

Thy Will Be Done

"Is God in the thing that you're in."
-Dr. Shaun Marler-

The Word says there is a way that seems right to a man but the end thereof is destruction. The Word also says that if we commit our ways to God that He will make straight our paths (Proverbs 3:6).

You can only go against the flow of God's will for your life for so long. You can only swim up river for so long; sooner or later strength will quit and you will be swept back. We must make sure that God is in the thing we are in. We must make sure we are in the will of God for our lives.

God has a perfect will for your life, so don't jump in a river and start swimming against the will of God for your life and then expect God to empower you to finish that course. Now, no matter how strong the current, no matter how hard or tough the opposition against you, no matter how great the odds - If God is in it He will empower you to finish your course.

Remember, you can do all things through Christ who strengthens you.

SECRET PLACE LIVING

Power Thought Thirty-Two

ENGAGING OTHERS

"If you want to lose friends quickly, start bragging about yourself. If you want to make and keep friends, start bragging about others."
-Unknown-

I read a book once that quoted a study on influence. In this report it stated, that the most introverted individual exerts an influence on over 10,000 people during the course of their life. Wow, imagine that! You and I are going to influence more than 10,000 people during the course of our lives. What a privilege, what an honour, but even more than this - what a responsibility we carry. To think that we influence over 10,000 people.

How many others are then influenced by these folk, and it goes on and on. It is the old throwing a stone into a pond and creating the ripple effect, the influence spirals out and on. Well, if we are going to influence this many people, and we are talking about the least amount (in actual fact the number will be far greater), then let's be a positive influence in their lives, let's influence people for God and for good.

Let us leave a positive impact and thereby change our world for the better. Be an influencer of good in someone's life. I dare you to make someone the richer for having known you. Even if the encounter is only a brief one. I dare you to make a difference by letting your *"words impart faith and grace to the hearers,"* as the Word says in Ephesians 4:29.

In getting along with others, 98% depends on our behaviour with others. *"Do to others as you would have them do to you,"* Jesus said in Luke 6:31. No matter how much work you can do, no matter how engaging your personality may be, you will not advance far in the business of life and ministry, if you cannot work through others.

And remember, a wise man once said, *"friendship flourishes at the fountain of forgiveness."*

Empowering you to win in life through Jesus Christ.

Power Thought Thirty-Three

JUST BE STILL

> *"The LORD is my shepherd, I shall not be in want.*
> *He makes me lie down in green pastures.*
> *He leads me beside quiet waters, he restores my soul.*
> *He guides me in paths of righteousness for his name's sake."*
> **-Psalm 23:1-3 (NIV)-**

Tragically, precious little in this hurried and hassled age promotes intimacy. We have become a body of people, who look more like a herd of cattle in a stampede, than a flock of God's people beside still waters and green pastures.

Our forefathers, it seems, knew how to spend time with God, to commune with the Almighty! Godliness is something that comes from God! We need to spend time with Him to learn from Him, to take His yoke which is easy to carry, and to lay down the heavy burdens of our heart.

My good friend Drummond says, *"If you give water out, you must go back to the source and allow God to fill you up again!"* We must re-learn the lost art of waiting on God, of spending time with Him so He can replenish our life and energy forces, and give us divine wisdom and instruction. Then we can grow and succeed in life, and be the best we can be for Him.

He is our Shepherd and desires to meet all our needs. Slow down and take the time to wait on God. Spend time listening to that still small voice of the Spirit and you will find rest for your souls.

Empowering you to win in life through Jesus Christ.

Power Thought Thirty-Four

Honour Your Man of God

"Render to all men their dues. [Pay] taxes to whom taxes are due, revenue to whom revenue is due, respect to whom respect is due, and honor to whom honor is due."
-Romans 13:7 (AMP)-

The word honour means: to respect, to revere, to treat with deference and submission and perform relevant duties to. Honouring your man of God is vital in the life of every born-again believer. Even as a Senior Pastor, it is a privilege for me to honour the men of God that I consider my spiritual fathers and mentors. They are life coaches to me on my spiritual journey to success, shining examples of excellence in ministry, men to whom I look for advice, prayer, guidance and leadership. The importance of a man such as this cannot be overstated.

Many of us would not be saved from the wrath to come, had it not been for the assistance, support and intervention of our Pastors. We would be ignorant of the Word, were it not for a man of God anointed to teach. Thank God for men who dare to teach the "Word of God", instead of the doctrines of man. To honour, trust and believe in your man of God, puts you in a place to be overtaken with favour.

> *"Believe in the LORD your God, and you shall be established; believe His prophets, and you shall prosper"* (2 Chronicles 20:20b NKJV).

I have found it is great to sow into the work of the ministry - God blesses those who do. But even more, I have found that when I have sown directly into a man of God's life, I have experienced a mighty return. I dare you today to buy your Pastor a gift, send him a card of appreciation, give him some money, do something that lets him know you honour him, respect him and love him. *"Honour all people. Love the brotherhood. Fear God. Honor the king."* (1 Peter 2:17, NKJV).

If you don't have a man of God in your life, find a good church that preaches the Word, join it and get yourself a Pastor. God has placed them in the body as gifts to you, to Shepherd your soul. When we give honour to our Pastor, we are giving Honour to God for the gift He has given us. As you honour God, He will honour you. In doing this, you will release unprecedented favour over your life.

Empowering you to win in life through Jesus Christ.

Power Thought Thirty-Five

MOVING ON

"God help me not to stew on things or beat myself up over dumb things I have done in the past."
-Dr. Shaun Marler-

You can't live in your yesterdays, you can't live in your tomorrows - you live now, so make this day count. The past will come to haunt you if you allow it. Pray, *"Lord I repent of my sins, I have called upon you in the day of trouble. Minister to me the comfort of the Holy Spirit, help me to stay my mind on you, as I trust you with my life and future. Jesus you are my rock, and my shelter in the day of trouble, and you deliver those who put their trust in you."*

Everyone has made mistakes and done dumb things, but if we stew on them, if we live there, we will never be free. We need to repent, change our way of thinking, change direction, put things right where we can, and move on into the things God has for us today.

I dare you to succeed this day, your future is great in Jesus.

Empowering you to win in life through Jesus Christ.

Power Thought Thirty-Six

HIS LOVE

"The only reason He extended His arms on the cross was so that He could embrace you!"
-Dr. Shaun Marler-

The word "embrace" means to hug, press to the bosom, accept willingly, to join, to encircle, surround, to receive gladly and eagerly, to take or clasp in the arms.

As they spread and nailed Jesus to the cross that day, He was dying for you, He was dying for me. The great passion of His heart was to love us, and set us free from the hell in our life, and the eternal hell to come.

Don't you know how much He loves you? How special and great a love, to go to the cross for you. Jesus was a real man with real feelings and a real body, He experienced real pain. Pain beyond what we could ever contemplate or imagine, and He did it all for us, for You!

Romans 8:31 says, *"if God be for you who can be against you."*

Empowering you to win in life through Jesus Christ.

Power Thought Thirty-Seven

HAVING FAITH TO SEE YOU THROUGH THE TOUGH TIMES

"Great faith is the product of great fights.
Great testimonies are the outcome of great tests.
Great triumphs can only come out of great trials."
-Smith Wigglesworth-

These are three of Smith Wigglesworth's pet sayings. I like to say, *"if you don't have a test you can't have a testimony."* Jesus said that in the world you will have temptations, tests, trials and tribulation. But He went on to say, *"be of good cheer because I have overcome the world"* (John 16:33). Jesus has defeated Satan and hell for us, and He hands victory to us on a plate. We have just got to receive by faith what the Lord has done. The Word says to fight the good fight of faith.

A good fight is one you win - and that is why when you fight-the-fight by faith, you win. Faith is the victory that overcomes the world. Jesus used His faith, the faith of God, to defeat and overcome the tricks and temptations of the devil.

He now says we can do the same, and hands us His faith which is tried and tested, with which to win and overcome. Satan the thief comes to steal, kill, and destroy, but Jesus has come that you might have life, and life more abundantly.

Yes, you will go through things on this planet during the course of your life. You will face many unpleasant and sometimes tragic circumstances and events. However, remember Jesus is there and He has given you faith to overcome and come through such situations.

By applying your faith in the circumstance, you will come through the time of testing and trial with a testimony to the glory of God.

Empowering you to win in life through Jesus Christ.

POWER THOUGHT THIRTY-EIGHT

GRATITUDE

"Gratitude is more than words. It's action and attitude."
-Dr. Shaun Marler-

Many people who order their lives rightly in all other ways, are kept in poverty by their lack of gratitude. Gratitude is an attitude we need to posses if we are to succeed in life. Gratitude is something we need to put into practice everyday in our life. "Practise the attitude of gratitude" - we need to constantly remind ourselves of how blessed we are. Put yourself in constant remembrance of the things God has done for you.

Psalm 34:1 says, *"I will bless the Lord at all times, His Praise shall continually be in my mouth."* This was one of the great secrets of King David's life. King David practised an attitude of gratitude, and God said of King David that he was a man after God's own heart.

It is easy to understand that the nearer we live to the source of wealth, the more wealth we shall receive; it is easy to understand that the soul that is always grateful, lives in closer touch with God, than the one which never looks to Him in thankful acknowledgement. The more gratefully we fix our minds on the supreme God when good things come to us, the more good things we will receive, and the more rapidly they will come.

We must learn to obey the universal laws of gratitude, because in doing so, you will stay in harmony with the laws of creative thought. God has put all these laws in place to keep the universe in balance. God is a God of order and discipline. These laws are for the benefit of all, and when we live by these laws, we in turn reap the rewards or blessings they produce.

Empowering you to win in life through Jesus Christ.

Power Thought Thirty-Nine

God Never Makes Mistakes

*"You are God's best. There is a sense of destiny in
your life because you are God's idea, His dream."*
-Dr. Shaun Marler-

Yes there is nobody else like you. Realize your potential, you were born for a reason, a purpose. God has an unbeatable plan for your life, and you know it on the inside. You were born for greatness, to be a child of the King.

It is time to awake to the plans of God, you were born again to win. You must discover your relationships, you must assume your God-given authority, it is time to use your power. Jesus said to wait on Him, *"tarry and you will be filled with power from on high"* (Luke 24:49), then you can access your wealth as a child of God.

I encourage you to believe in your destiny. Yes, my friend, you have a destiny, and remember God loves you.

Empowering you to win in life through Jesus Christ.

Power Thought Forty

IF IT'S UNACCEPTABLE, DON'T ACCEPT IT

"If it's unacceptable, don't accept it."
-John Parolin-

In our Men's Breakfast on Saturday, the topic of discussion was 'raising the standard'. My brother-in-law, John, said his old boss who is now retired, had a favourite saying and it goes like this, *"If it's unacceptable, don't accept it."* John said he now makes that one of his daily themes.

All too often in life we settle for second best, all too often we settle for a lower standard than what we really desire or hope for. Some people long to see a greater victory, a better outcome, a standard of excellence, yet never get to see their dreams realized, and become frustrated to the point where they lower their hopes.

The Bible tells us that *"hope deferred makes the heart sick"* (Proverbs 13:12). If we think of sick ground or sour ground, we know it's ability to grow and produce is diminished or even neutralized. A farmer will plough his ground, fertilise it and sometimes, he will even grow a crop, just to be ploughed back in, for the express purpose of refreshing and redepositing minerals and elements that have been depleted through continual use.

If you have lowered your standards today, if your dreams have been stolen from you, if you feel depleted today, let me encourage you. First, lift up again the standard of excellence, be determined to give life your best effort and expect life's best back in return. Keep moving forward; don't settle for anything unacceptable.

When the desire comes, it is a tree of life (Proverbs 13:12), keep pushing forward towards your dreams and practice the 'Praising Principle'. Remember, your best is yet to come.

Empowering you to win in life through Jesus Christ.

Power Thought Forty-One

DIVINE INTERRUPTIONS

*"Be open for God to interrupt your day,
as God interruptions lead to great opportunities."*
-Dr. Shaun Marler-

In life we are frequently interrupted, some times those interruptions are not just life's coincidences. No, they are often much more than that - they can be divine interruptions that help us discover our wealth and use our gifts. Most of the miracles of Jesus were divine interruptions. We need to be sensitive to God, ask *"Father is this you interrupting me or just an attack from the enemy?"*

Remember people are paramount to Jesus. You have God's ability to be a life changer everyday, you can make a difference in somebody's life today. Ephesians 6:8 shows us that if we make things happen for others, God will make good things happen for us. In Matthew 8:1, we see a situation where Jesus allowed Himself to be interrupted, and as a result, a great miracle of cleansing took place in a leper's life. Further into the chapter another miracle of great healing occurs, when Jesus allowed a solider to interrupt His travels.

Go on I dare you, I challenge you today, the next time a little interruption comes along to mess up your busy day or schedule. Don't just get annoyed, but stop to see if this is not a God given opportunity for you to be used of God, to let your gifts flow, to make a difference and add some value to someone's life.

Empowering you to win in life through Jesus Christ.

Power Thought Forty-Two

COME APART BEFORE YOU COME APART

"Come apart before you come apart."
-Dr. Shaun Marler-

My good friend the late Drummond Thom said. *"If you give water out, you must go back to the source and allow God to fill you up again."* Take time to allow God to speak, inspire, fill and recharge your batteries. We must learn to wait on God.

Try this: Choose a time and a place that is best for you, the only requirement, is that you separate yourself from distractions, from the noise and confusion of life. This is your time to hear from God, you must come apart and rest awhile, for if you do not come apart and rest, you will eventually come apart. I have witnessed this happen to friends of mine. I have witnessed people of God suffer, and burn out.

I am also speaking from personal experience here. So remember, come apart before you come apart. The Sabbath day was made for man to rest, because Father knows best.

Empowering you to win in life through Jesus Christ.

Power Thought Forty-Three

God's Spirit Knows- Look Before You Leap

"But you have an unction from the Holy One, and you know all things."
-1 John 2:20-

The Holy Spirit knows how to get you there safer and faster, because God's Word says, *"there is a way that seems right to a man, but the end there of is destruction."* The word says in Psalm 37:23, *"the steps of a good man are ordered by the Lord"*, notice it says steps not leaps.

When I was young, my mum always told me to look before you leap, and so when it came to jumping into lakes and rivers, I have always heeded this helpful piece of advice. Yet, sorry to say, I have not always applied this wisdom to all of life, and as such have had to at times learn the hard way. Sometimes I have jumped into relationships, business decisions and other things, only to regret that I did not look before I leaped.

You may want to get to where you are going as fast as you can but if you are not using God's wisdom, waiting on Him and doing it His way, you could be headed for a crash. My prayer for you today is this, pray and agree with me;

Lord I thank you for the leading of the Holy Spirit in my friend's life. Forgive us where we have wasted time and money and energy doing things our way. Holy Spirit be our guide today, please step into our lives and lead us one step at a time into the wonderful things you have planned and have in store for us. Please be our guide, our teacher, comforter and friend. Thank you Father in Jesus' name, for providing us with this wonderful guide and friend, the Holy Spirit. Lord we open up ourselves in Jesus' name to receive your wisdom and divine guidance for we know you have a plan for our lives and our best interests at heart. In Jesus' Name, AMEN!

Now remember to look before you leap, or you may not like what you are going to land yourself in.

Empowering you to win in life through Jesus Christ.

POWER THOUGHT FORTY-FOUR

WE MUST DECREASE SO HE CAN INCREASE

"Jesus was the personification of humility in the midst of His unlimited power."
-Dr. Shaun Marler-

Our goal should be, to be like our teacher Jesus. In Philippians 2:5-9, we learn that Jesus made Himself of no reputation but took on Himself the form of a servant. He humbled Himself and became obedient (He became obedient, it was not automatic) unto death, even the death of the cross. Luke 14:27 says *"And whosoever does not bear his cross and come [or go] after Jesus, cannot be His Disciple"*.

Jesus emptied Himself, we must empty our self and get full of Him. John the Baptist said *"I must decrease, while He increases"*. We must decrease so He can increase in us. A disciple is a disciplined follower; it takes discipline to be a disciple, that's delayed gratification.

Isaiah 8:16: *"Bind up the testimony; seal the law among my disciples"*. The Hebrew word for disciple means: one who is instructed, accustomed, learned, taught and used. In the Greek it means "A learner", one who is permeated or soaked with the knowledge of

Christ, and from this, comes into understanding of Him. In Matthew 10:16 is says, that Disciples were to be shrewd and innocent. Shrewd means wise, thoughtful (full of thoughts of God and considerate). They were to be discreet, implying a cautious character. To go forward with wisdom and to be led by the Spirit of God.

Empowering you to win in life through Jesus Christ.

Power Thought Forty-Five

Born Twice, Die Once

"If you are born once, you will die twice.
If you are born twice you will die once."
-Dr. Shaun Marler-

Wow! Think about this, the bible says you must be born again or you will never get to see the Kingdom of God (John 3:3).

"Jesus answered and said unto him, Verily, verily, I say unto thee, except a man be born again, he cannot see the kingdom of God".

Jesus said in John 3:5 *"Verily, verily, I say unto thee, except a man be born of water* (natural birth) *and of the Spirit* (spiritual rebirth), *he cannot enter into the kingdom of God".*

John 3:6-7 *"That which is born of the flesh is flesh; and that which is born of the Spirit is spirit. Marvel not* (don't be amazed or wonder how can this be) *that I said unto thee, Ye must be born again".*

Jesus here was speaking about a second birth, not a natural birth, but a spiritual birth. This second birth takes place by the Spirit of God in your heart, your inner being, your spirit man, making you born again.

> John 3:16 *"For God so loved* (God is a God of love) *the world* (that's you, me, everybody, everywhere, every time, every race, every colour and creed, the whole world, all people), *that he gave* (love gives, forgives and always lives, it's eternal) *his only begotten Son* (Jesus, God incarnate in the flesh, Emmanuel), *that whosoever believes* (entrust your spiritual wellbeing to Christ, have faith) *in him should not perish, but have everlasting* (never coming to an end) *life* (the God kind of life)".

I encourage you today where you are, whatever state or circumstance you are in, give your life to God today. Get born again and live forever!

Empowering you to win in life through Jesus Christ.

Power Thought Forty-Six

Words, Words, Words...

"For out of the abundance of the heart the mouth speaks."
-Matthew 12:34b-

When you pray, watch out for both hasty words and too many words (Mat 6:7). The secret of acceptable praying is a prepared heart (Ps 141:1-2) because the mouth speaks what the heart contains (Mat 12:34). If we pray only to impress people, we will not get through to God. The author of Pilgrim's Progress, John Bunyan, wrote. *"In prayer, it is better to have a heart without words, than words without a heart."*

Ecc 5:2, *"Be not rash with thy mouth, and let not thine heart be hasty to utter any thing before God: for God is in heaven, and thou upon earth: therefore let thy words be few."*

Empowering you to win in life through Jesus Christ.

Power Thought Forty-Seven

Take Another Drink

"And they waited for me as for the rain; and they opened their mouth wide as for the latter rain."
-Job 29:23-

If you are thirsty and dry, lift your hands to the sky and worship the King. Rain doesn't fall, gravity pulls it down. It is your passion and it is your hunger, that draws God to you. Psalm 72:6 says *"He shall come down like rain upon the mown grass, as showers that water the earth."* Mown grass speaks of a prepared and maintained field, it is ready.

When you give out continually, you can get dry yourself. The more you minister, the more you need to be ministered to. If you constantly give water out, you need to go back to the source and be refreshed and refilled. Psalm 72:19, *"And blessed be His glorious name forever and let the whole earth be filled with His glory, amen and amen."* Draw near to God and He will draw near to you.

SECRET PLACE LIVING

Empowering you to win in life through Jesus Christ.

POWER THOUGHT FORTY-EIGHT

DESTINY IS A CHOICE

"Destiny is not a matter of chance, it is a matter of choice; it is not a thing to be waited for, it is a thing to be achieved."
-Dr. Shaun Marler-

"But Shaun, you don't know me! I have tried every formula in the book. I just keep failing; I don't have what it takes to succeed." Well if that is what you are thinking, you need to change what you are thinking. God says you can fulfil your destiny and no one has a right to stop you.

God told Joshua in chapter 1 verse 5, "There shall not any man be able to stand before you all the days of your life. As I was with Moses, so I will be with you. I will not fail you, nor will I forsake you" (Josh 1:5).

God had told Moses in the book of Exodus (Ex 3:12), when Moses claimed he wasn't qualified, to go before Pharaoh to demand the release of God's people, that He (God) was with Moses. In other words, it doesn't matter who you are, if God is with you, all that matters is who God is and what God can do.

That's the great thing about God's success formula. It is not based on our abilities; it is based on God's abilities. We may be inadequate in a dozen different ways, but the One who is with us is more than enough. In order to fulfil our destiny, we have to make a decision to act on and believe God's word.

Make a decision today that with God's help, with His ability, you will fulfil your purpose in life. Joshua 1:7 says *"Be strong and very courageous, that you may do according to all the law which Moses my servant commanded you. Turn not from it to the right hand or to the left that you may prosper wherever you go."*

Wow, now that's a powerful promise. If we take the bold step to act on and trust the Word of God, if we take the bold step to obey the word of God, live our life by the principles of God's word, then God Himself takes responsibility for our success and prosperity.

I dare you today to believe in your divine destiny. I dare you today to obey the Word of God. I dare you today to make a quality decision to achieve your purpose in life, and do the necessary thing to make it happen.

Empowering you to win in life through Jesus Christ.

POWER THOUGHT FORTY-NINE

AGAINST THE ODDS

"And he said, the things which are impossible with men are possible with God."
-Luke 18:27-

Aerodynamically the bumble bee shouldn't be able to fly, but the bumble bee doesn't know this, so it goes on flying anyway. It takes courage to fly, when the circumstances and every one around, is screaming in your ears you can't. It takes courage to stand on and continue to believe the Word of God, when all hell is arrayed against you. But once you make the decision to do it, you will be ready to activate God's three part formula for success.

Make the decision that you will win, make the decision that you will beat the odds; make the decision that you will achieve victory in life through Jesus Christ. You are not alone, God is with you today and He is on your side. Like the bumble bee, He will give you the ability to succeed in the face of impossible odds.

Joshua 1:8 *"This book of law shall not depart out of your mouth; but you shall meditate therein day and night that you may observe and do according to all that is written in it. For then you shall make your way prosperous and then you will have good success."*

In the Amplified bible, it says if we do this we will deal wisely and have good success. I like that, deal wisely! So what are the 3 steps God gives us here in this verse?

1. Keep your heart and mouth full of the Word of God.
2. Meditate (speak, dream, mutter, imagine, think, get a mental picture) on the Word day and night.
3. Observe and do (obey) according to all that is written in it.

There they are, three simple steps directly from the mouth of God. Steps that enabled Joshua to conquer the land of Canaan and bring Israel into their inheritance. Steps that will enable you to live like the conqueror God designed you to be.

Empowering you to win in life through Jesus Christ.

Power Thought Fifty

EVERY TOMORROW HAS TWO HANDLES

*"Every tomorrow has two handles. You can take hold of the handle of anxiety or the handle of enthusiasm.
Upon your choice so will the day be."*
-Dr. Shaun Marler-

"Do not let this Book of the Law depart from your mouth;" (Joshua 1:8a). That's the first element of supernatural success God gives us in this verse. I like to say it this way, make a decision this day and every day to talk the word.

Deuteronomy 6:7 says, *"...Speak the word when you sit at home, speak the word when you walk along the road, talk the word when you lie down and talk the word when you get up."* Be consistent, talk and speak the word all the time, all the day!

Romans 10:17 declares that, *"Faith comes by hearing and hearing by the word of God"*.

In Luke 6:45 Jesus said, *"...out of the abundance of the heart the mouth speaks"*. If you worry about your finances, your job, your health, or your family all day, that will be your focus and you will fill your heart with fear and anxiety. To change what is coming out of your mouth, you must change your focus. Fill your heart with the word and your mouth will get in line. Your answer is in God's word in your heart and mouth.

Upon your choice so will the day be.

Empowering you to win in life through Jesus Christ.

Power Thought Fifty-One

FAITH IS NEEDED FOR THE IMPOSSIBLE

"Faith is needed for the impossible, and so you dare to act on the Word, as though the impossible had become a possibility, a reality."
-E.W. Kenyon-

The third step in God's formula for success involves action. We must act as though the Word we have been speaking, talking and meditating about, is true, even when the circumstances seem to say otherwise.

Jesus said, *"The things which are impossible with men are possible with God."* (Luke 18:27). We have to act like we have already received the answer. Right here is where a lot of people miss it, because they fail to act on God's Word even though they know it works. You may have been studying God's Word for years. You may know how to live by faith better than anybody around, but if you only know and fail to act, or do God's Word, you will miss the rewards. Remember it is not what you know, but rather what you know and act on, that brings the victory into manifestation.

Mark 11:22-24, *"Have faith in God. For truly I say to you that whosoever shall say to this mountain, 'Be thou removed and be cast into the sea', and shall not doubt in his heart but shall believe that those things he says with his mouth shall come to pass, he shall have just what he says. Therefore I say unto you, whatsoever things you desire, when you pray, believe that you receive them, and then you shall have them."*

Notice Jesus didn't say you should believe you receive when you see it. He said to believe you receive, when you pray. John G. Lake said, *"Beloved, it is not our long prayers but our believing God that gets the answer."*

Now if you follow His instructions, how do you think you should act? You should act like you have it now, you have your victory now, and you have your answer now! Do something you could not do before. Lift that arm, move that leg, bend that back! Rejoice, be happy! Praise God for the Victory now, thank Him for answering your prayers before you see it with your eyes and then you shall have it!

Empowering you to win in life through Jesus Christ.

Power Thought Fifty-Two

FAITH

"A little faith will bring your soul to heaven; A great faith will bring heaven to your soul."
-Charles Spurgeon-

Faith is more than mental assent; faith believes what the Word says, even though sight and feelings may be saying something different.

One of the greatest enemies of real faith is a thing called, "mental assent". People who act in mental assent say they believe the Word, but when the pressure is on, they go to pieces and start speaking fear and unbelief. You can tell if they really believe the Word or not, by what is coming out of their mouth. If they're questioning God's love, His ability, or just plain speaking the opposite to what God says, then you know they were in mental assent and not faith. When you are in faith, regardless of the circumstances, your heart is fixed trusting in the Lord.

Philippians 4:7 says, *"And the peace of God that passes all understanding, shall keep your hearts and minds in Christ Jesus."*

People in mental assent just plain don't act on the Word when problems arise. Mental assent says, *"I believe the bible from cover to cover. I believe I am healed by the stripes of Jesus."* However, when sickness actually comes or attacks, it stops saying, *"I am healed,"* and starts saying, *"I am sick."*

Faith doesn't care what the symptoms are; it doesn't care what the circumstances may be! It isn't moved by the banker's or doctor's report. It is only moved by what it believes! And it believes what God said is true, and confesses it! Faith in God's Word will change the symptoms. It will change the bank account. It will bring money to get the bills paid. Faith will turn defeat into victory. It is God's success formula! But remember, you have to give that faith an opportunity to work. Give it some time, to produce the results it was designed by God to produce. You have to keep God's Word in your mouth and meditate on it in your heart. You have to be obedient to what God says, by faith and patience inherit the promises. As you do these things, you will make your way prosperous and you will have good success.

Empowering you to win in life through Jesus Christ.

POWER THOUGHT FIFTY-THREE

SUCCESS IN LIFE

*"If you want something you have never had,
you have to do something you have never done!"*
-Dr. Shaun Marler-

Now think about that again. A definition of insanity, is to do the same thing over and over and expect a different result. How much do you want success in life? Enough to change what you are saying, or enough to change what you are doing, or enough to change what you are focusing your attention on?

You have to act on God's Word even when everything is telling you it won't work. If you want it that much, the Word of God guarantees you will find success in life. The Word, or bible, tells us that God's success is good success. There are two kinds of success, good success that brings happiness with it, and the kind that brings sorrow.

Too many people have succeeded at the expense of their health, or family, or relationships. That's not what God wants, He says in Proverbs 10:22 *"The blessing of the Lord makes one rich! And He adds no sorrow with it."* Now that's the kind we want! The word "blessing", used here is a Hebrew word for prosperity! The word, "rich" used here, means to grow rich or, to make one rich! Isn't that excellent? *"And He adds no sorrow with it"*, that word means, *"painful toil, mind or body, hard labour or sorrow."*

I will warn you, Satan won't like it if you choose the way of success. He will do whatever he can to try to stop you having, or entering God's best for your life. He also knows what tactics to use against you to try to distract you from God's will. His goal is to stop your dreams, by stopping your faith. Satan knows faith will bring you answers to your prayers, and he will use all he has to get you to stop believing God's Word! He will put thoughts of doubt into your mind, thoughts of fear and worry. Anything opposite to God's Word is what the devil will tell you. Don't listen to him; don't let those thoughts become yours, even though they are in your head. They don't become yours, unless you believe them and take them by speaking them.

Don't speak the problem; don't let the fear into your heart. Don't dwell on what the devil is saying, but only dwell on what God is saying!

Empowering you to win in life through Jesus Christ.

Power Thought Fifty-Four

BELIEVE

*"I am not moved by what I see. I am not moved by what I feel.
I am only moved by what I believe."*
-Smith Wigglesworth-

If God's Word says you are forgiven, then you are forgiven, if God's Word says your needs are met, then your needs are met. If God's Word says you are healed, you are healed. If you don't let go of God's Word, but keep it in your heart and mouth, then you can't lose.

There is no force the devil can bring against you that can overthrow the Word of God. God's Word will make you a victor every time. So if you have been wanting good success and it has been eluding you, quit wondering if you have what it takes to succeed and remember instead, who lives in you. Then turn to the Word and put God's success formula to work in your life. Start talking it, start thinking it, start doing it! You can believe all day long that the Bible is true- and that's to your credit- but what the Bible says will never affect your life in a personal way, until you start acting on God's Word.

Do not worry or fret that God has given more faith to others than He has to you. Rest assured in the fact that God has imparted enough faith to you, to make sure you are covered from head to toe! Faith counts the thing done, before anything has happened. Remember, no promise of God can fail to be fulfilled. (Luke 1:37).

Empowering you to win in life through Jesus Christ.

Power Thought Fifty-Five

Desire the Milk of the Word

"Desire the sincere milk of the word, that you may grow through it."
-1 Peter 2:2-

Here the word of God is telling us to have a desire for God's pure truth, found in the Bible. We should make it a daily practice to feed on the good Word of God. As we can see from this scripture, this desire and habit will cause us to grow. That is what God wants; God wants mature Christians that are ready to serve Him. As we grow, we will become powerful in faith and powerful in spirit, which will work out in our lives.

Some people wonder why they can't have faith for healing. Yet they feed their bodies three hot meals a day and their spirits one cold snack a week. Just imagine if an elite athlete only fed their body once a week. It would not matter how talented or gifted they were, it wouldn't matter how hard or often they trained, soon they would be left behind in the field.

We as Christians, need to learn that our strength is in the Word, and as we feed on it, we will digest it, and it will go down and nourish our inner man. This Word in us will transform us and cause us to walk in the Spirit. When we are in the Spirit we are unconquerable, going from victory to victory, our life becomes hidden with Christ in God. The secret of having more faith is to know more about God, and God has revealed Himself to us through His Word. Our work is to know Him and He is to be found in His Word, for He and His Word are one.

Paul said; *"That I may know Him and the power of His resurrection"* (Philippians 3:10),

Empowering you to win in life through Jesus Christ.

Power Thought Fifty-Six

DO THE FEARED JOBS FIRST!

"I can do all things through Christ which strengtheneth me."
-*Philippians 4:13*-

One of the greatest ways I have learned to maximize my days is by doing the feared jobs first. By this, I mean those jobs you don't want to do. Those phone calls you don't want to make. Those activities you wish you didn't have to do at all. Do them first, tackle them first up in your day. In so doing, you get them out of the way early and then your energy can be put into the work you love, without the drain in the back of your mind of the thing you have been dreading, or fearing to do. You can prioritize your day, making a list of what needs to be done and ticking them off as you go. In so doing, you can look back over your day or week and be encouraged by all you have achieved.

Proverbs 27:23 says, *"Be you diligent to know the state of your flocks* (business, ministry, family), *and look well to your herds* (people, ministry, possessions.)*"*

Empowering you to win in life through Jesus Christ.

Power Thought Fifty-Seven

First Seek the Kingdom of God

"Make every day, a successful day for it is the successful days that make you rich."
-Dr. Shaun Marler-

You can't get rich on failure days, but you can't fail to get rich on successful days. So then, make today successful, full of success, seek first the Kingdom of God and your day will be successful. Put God first in all you do, and God will make you to prosper! That's God's solemn promise, His covenant to you!

You can't bring back yesterday, you can only fully maximize today. Live life with purpose, live life with urgency. Don't live in "Woulda! Coulda! Shoulda!" Forget what lays behind, yesterday is gone, learn from your mistakes so as to not repeat them, but don't live in your mistakes, move on, live in today, not yesterday. Believe for a better day, dream of a better day. Dream of victory.

The number one form of failure in all our lives is excuses. Get over your own excuses, you were born to overcome. Propel yourself forward to get results. You can't buy back yesterday, but you can own today, you can make today a winning day, thereby affecting your tomorrows.

Your tomorrows are established by what you do today. Take care of today and tomorrow will take care of itself. It is time for you to step into what God has for your life. Remember, "*This is the day that the Lord has made, let us rejoice and be glad in it!*"

Empowering you to win in life through Jesus Christ.

Power Thought Fifty-Eight

YOU HAVE THE CAPACITY TO THINK BIG

"For as a person thinks in their heart, so are they." Or, "As a man thinketh in his heart, so is he."
-Proverbs 23:7a-

You have the capacity to think big. Only big thinkers will achieve big things. If you can conceive things in your mind and see them in your imagination, you can receive them. "Conceive it, and you can achieve it!" God wants you to think BIG. I have never known God to give a person a small vision. The visions that come from God, may ask you to do small things, to see your heart, your willingness or your obedience, but when God gives you a vision to achieve something, it is usually always beyond what you could do in your own strength, resources or abilities. God wants you to trust in Him, rely upon Him and look to Him for your supply and source. Remember, God is your resource. If you can think big, then you can do big, because your God is big and it is His strength, His power and His ability, that will go to work on your behalf.

Think big and do big things for God!

Empowering you to win in life through Jesus Christ.

Power Thought Fifty-Nine

God Meets All Your Needs

*"Never speak of times as being hard
or of business conditions as being doubtful."*
-Dr. Shaun Marler-

Times may be hard, or business conditions tough, for those on a competitive plane, but they are never that way for you, because God has promised in Philippians 4:19, to meet all your needs according to His riches in glory. You don't have to compete for things in the competitive plane or realm. You move by faith into a whole new realm or plane, and receive of God's abundance. You can create what you want and operate above fear.

When others are having hard times and poor business, you will find the greatest opportunities. You are being supplied by a different realm and it is exhaustless. Train yourself to think and look upon the world as something which is becoming, which is growing, which is increasing. Always speak in terms of advancement. To do otherwise is to deny your faith, and to deny your faith is to lose it. Remember your supply is not confined to what is seen or already in existence. Your supply is from the limitless source of God's glory, what is becoming, what is increasing. You don't serve a limited God. But you serve Father, Son and Holy Spirit, unlimited.

Empowering you to win in life through Jesus Christ.

Power Thought Sixty

YOUR BEST IS YET TO COME

"Don't dig up in doubt what you plant in faith."
-Dr. Shaun Marler-

Remember, better is the end of a thing than the beginning thereof. Your best is yet to come. You are heading for a better day.

There is a spiritual law in Genesis 8:22, that tells us that while the earth remains, seed time and harvest shall not cease. I want to encourage you today to keep pressing in, keep believing, keep standing on God's Word, don't quit, don't give up. Remember, the Word works when you work the Word, so keep working that Word!

If you don't quit, in due season, what you have been believing for will come to pass. So make up your mind now that quitting is not an option. Hold that dream, that Word, steadfast in your heart. When the Word is planted in the good soil of your heart, it always produces a harvest. The process of seed time and harvest, is not just a natural process, it is a supernatural process. The most powerful seed is the Word of God. The entire universe was framed and is held up by the Word of God's power. God's Word will produce in your life what it was designed to produce, so hold that thought, hold that dream of victory, of greatness, and don't let it go.

You are a winner in Him!

Empowering you to win in life through Jesus Christ.

FINAL NOTE FROM THE AUTHOR

This is my first book of a six-book series. I pray that these power thoughts have been a real blessing and encouragement to your life. Remember Jeremiah 29:1.

> *"For I know the plans I have for you," declares the Lord, "plans to prosper you and not to harm you, plans to give you hope and a future. Then you will call on me and come and pray to me, and I will listen to you. You will seek me and find me when you seek me with all your heart"* (Jeremiah 29:11-13, NIV).

Once again, I encourage every one of you to find your secret place. A quiet place where you can get intimate with God by getting intimate with His Word and Spirit. Learn to lean on God daily. Love on God and let Him love on you. Allow God to speak into your spirit daily, by His Spirit through His life-giving Word.

I leave you with two of my favourite verses from the Bible.

> *"Keep this Book of the Law always on your lips; meditate on it day and night, so that you may be careful to do everything written in it. Then you will be prosperous and successful"* (Joshua 1:8).

> *"Beloved, I wish above all things that you may prosper and be in health, even as thy soul prospers"* (3 John 2).

PARTNERSHIP

Help Pastor Shaun to help others, by becoming a Harvest Partner in this great work of spreading the gospel and loving others.

Please email general@whm.org.au and become a World Harvest partner today!

For other information and a complete list of products, or to find out how you can partner with the ministry of Dr Shaun Marler and World Harvest Ministries, contact:
P.O. Box 90, Bald Hills, 4036

Queensland, Australia
Phone: +61 7 3261 4555
(9am – 4:30pm EST Aust)

Web: whm.org.au
Email: general@whm.org.au

Facebook: www.facebook.com/worldharvestmin
Facebook: www.facebook.com/ShaunMarlerWHM
Twitter: twitter.com/world_harvest
Youtube: youtube.com/worldharvestlife
Instagram: @i_harvest

Natural Superfoods is partnering with World Harvest Ministries. 10% of their income goes to support our mission programs, helping to feed widows, orphans and reaching the lost for Christ.

Natural Superfoods and Co have great products for detoxing and helping people maintain optimum health. These products, like their 'Enlighten Supergreens', which are a unique proprietary blend of powerful, natural, organic superfoods, designed to boost your immune system. Some of which can be used as a great daily supplement for general well-being. Always consult a healthcare professional before using this or any dietary supplement.

If you desire to purchase any of these amazing supplements, you can do so by visiting their domain:

naturalsuperfoodsco.com

Raw plant based superfoods to support balanced healthy living.

10% of your purchase will go to supporting the ministry. In this way, your own health can benefit at the same time you will be helping us to help others.

'Discipline', just one word but a powerful ingredient to achieve life's targets.

Be blessed!
Ps. Shaun.

NOTES

I have added a few blank pages here for you to write down your own thoughts, inspirations and revelations, as you read, study and meditate the power thoughts in this book. What you learn, what you glean, teach others that they too may grow in the Lord and become very effective in life and ministry. I will leave you with one last scripture.

"For as he thinks in his heart, so is he."
(Proverbs 23:7a)

NOTES

NOTES

NOTES

Also by Dr. Shaun Marler

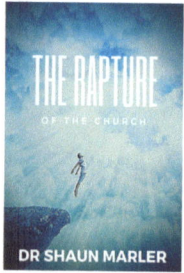

The Rapture of the Church
This book will help you prepare for the next great event on the Christian calendar. Learn what the word 'Rapture' means -God's ability to catch up people alive to His presence. Timelines included, pointing to when we can expect this event to occur and much more!

Life Changing Principles For Victorious Living
Life Changing Principles for Victorious Living is a must read! You will find keys to unlock your life in Christ.

Praise Power
Everything in your life is subject to change. God's will for your life is that it changes for the better. How do you get there? Through praise in the Word, because praise is the verbal expression of Faith and Faith is the language of Heaven.

SECRET PLACE LIVING

Fast Way to Power
In this book you will learn the secret to the presence and power of God, in the lives of some of His Great Generals. You will learn the ABC's that they knew that enabled them to walk in God's miracle healing power. You will learn to flow in the miracle life, by discovering the fast way to power! Plus amazing end-time prophecies.

Divine Healing 101
This is a how-to book with examples, teachings and personal testimonies, that prove it is God's will that you not only be healed, but walk in divine health, all the days of your life.

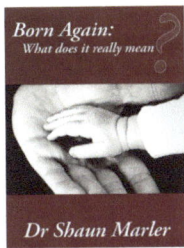

Born Again; What does it really mean?
This mini book is a must have! You will learn how you can accept Jesus Christ as Saviour and what it really means to be born again. Discover how you can enjoy all the blessings will now belong to you!

These books and other titles are available on Amazon as well as other online bookstores around the world!

ABOUT THE AUTHOR

Dr Shaun Marler is the Senior Pastor and co-founder with his wife Kerrie of World Harvest Ministries, an international organisation based in Queensland, Australia, World Harvest Ministries is committed to carrying out the Great Commission of Jesus our Lord. Taking the healing word to the nations and feeding the hungry, visiting prisoners, clothing the naked, visiting the widows and orphans in their affliction, and preaching the Good News to the poor.

World Harvest Ministries currently has programs in Australia, Africa and India, where the poor and destitute are given free medical treatment, orphan homes where children are fed, accommodated and educated, a ministry to widows who have been abandoned by society and a program to feed people with leprosy.

A portion of the proceeds of the sale of this book goes towards this valuable work, which is making a huge difference in the lives of others!